The Magdalene Path

A Rose Pocket Sanctuary Series™ - Volume III

The Magdalene Path
Rose Pocket Sanctuary Series™ — Volume III

This Pocket Sanctuary is intended for personal spiritual enrichment and reflection. It is not meant to replace professional, medical, or therapeutic guidance.

Published by Rooted Hound Press
Vienna, New Jersey
rootedhoundpress.com

Cover design by Rooted Hound Press.

ISBN 978-1-969687-09-9

Printed in the United States of America.

First Edition: 2025

For those who rise even when the dawn feels far away.

Table of Contents

The Rose Series™ – Pocket Sanctuaries

A devotional collection exploring the Rose Lineage, the feminine path of remembrance, and the quiet wisdom that awakens the soul.

Volume I
The Rose Codex
A guide to the ancient symbolism of the Rose and the heart-centered path of awakening.

Volume II
Mary Magdalene: A Sanctuary of Remembrance
A restoration of the Magdalene's voice, presence, and feminine wisdom.

Volume III

The Magdalene Path
An embodied guide to living the Rose teachings through daily devotion, truth, softness, and inner remembrance.

Forthcoming Volumes
The Magdalene Path: Daily Practices
The Lost Feminine Gospels
The Rose Priestess
The Rose at the End of the World
(Additional volumes will continue to unfold.)

Preface: Walking the Path of Remembering

The Magdalene Path is not a path of perfection. It is a path of returning—to yourself, to your truth, to the quiet wisdom that rises beneath the noise of life.

Where the *Rose Codex* introduced the lineage, and *Mary Magdalene: A Sanctuary of Remembrance* restored the voice of the Beloved, this third volume invites you into the living, breathing practice of the Rose.

Mary did not walk her journey through certainty. She walked it through devotion—honest, trembling, human devotion that held her steady through confusion, grief, loss, love, and awakening.

This Sanctuary is not a history book or a set of instructions. It is a companion for the days when you feel lost, for the mornings you rise before you are ready, for the moments when your heart whispers truth your mind has not yet learned to understand.

The Magdalene Path is lived in the small choices—the breath you take before reacting, the moment you stay when fear tells you to run, the quiet honesty you offer yourself in the car, the softness you choose instead of hardening.

This book is here to walk with you in those moments. To remind you that your unfolding is sacred, your trembling is holy, and your becoming is already underway.

Welcome to the Path. May it meet you gently and guide you toward the rose blooming within you.

HOW TO USE THIS SANCTUARY

This Pocket Sanctuary is meant to be read slowly.

You do not need to complete it in one sitting. You do not need to take notes or "keep up." You do not need any prior knowledge of the Rose, Mary Magdalene, or spiritual symbolism.

Simply move at the pace that feels natural to you.

Each section offers:

✦ A Teaching

A gentle explanation of the Rose's wisdom and how it applies to your everyday life.

✦ An Affirmation

A sentence to anchor the lesson into your heart.

✦ A Journaling Prompt

A doorway for deeper inner exploration.

There is no right way to use this Sanctuary. You may:

> read one section a day

> move intuitively between pages

return to certain teachings when needed

use this as part of a morning ritual

keep it by your bedside

read it quietly with tea

tuck it into your bag as a reminder of your path

Let this Sanctuary be what it was designed to be:

A small companion. A gentle teacher. A reminder that your soul unfolds one petal at a time.

When you're ready, turn the page and enter the first teaching.

SECTION 1 — When the Light Feels Far Away

There are days when the lamp goes dim,
when the heart feels hollow,
when faith curls in on itself
like a frightened animal.
Do not fear these days.
Even Mary knew them—
the empty mornings,
the unanswered questions,
the ache of believing without seeing.
The path does not begin in certainty.
It begins in longing.
It begins in the quiet place inside you
that whispers, "There must be more than this."

People imagine the spiritual path begins with a moment of
revelation—a clear sign, a surge of knowing, a brightening
of the inner world. But the truth is softer. Most journeys
begin in the dimness. Mary's did too. Before she became the
one who stayed, the one who understood, the one who rose
before dawn, there was a moment long before all of that—a
moment where the light felt far away, and she didn't yet
know her place in the story.

I've had moments like that myself—moments when I was
sitting in my car in a grocery store parking lot, hands on the
wheel, unable to make myself go inside. Nothing dramatic

had happened. I was just tired. The kind of tired that makes the world feel heavier than it should. I remember whispering, "I don't feel connected to anything lately." And in that moment, nothing shifted. I didn't see a sign. I didn't suddenly understand anything. I let myself sit there, overwhelmed and breathing slowly because that was all I could do.

It wasn't until later—hours after that moment had passed—that something inside me softened. Not a breakthrough, not clarity…just a gentle realization that the heaviness I felt wasn't necessarily a dead end. It might have been pointing to something within me that needed more care, more honesty, more space. I didn't have answers. But I could feel the beginning of a truth rising: sometimes the moments when we feel cut off are not failures. They're invitations. Openings. A quiet pull toward what wants to be seen.

The Magdalene Path often begins here—when the light feels far away, and the heart aches for something it can't yet name. That ache is not a sign that you're lost. It's the first whisper that you're beginning.

Affirmation

"When the light feels far, I listen to the longing within me."

Journaling Prompt

Write about a time when the light felt distant—when you felt tired, disconnected, or unsure. What was the longing beneath that moment? What was your soul quietly asking for?

SECTION 2 — The Courage to Stay When You Want to Run

There are moments when the ground shifts,
when the heart trembles,
when you feel the urge to retreat
from your own truth.
Staying feels impossible.
Leaving feels easier.
But somewhere inside,
a steadier voice whispers,
"Don't abandon yourself now."
Staying is not stillness.
It is devotion wearing its bravest face.

Mary stayed at the foot of the cross when nearly everyone else fled. She didn't stay because she was fearless. She stayed because something within her refused to abandon love, even when love led her through the darkest valley. Her courage was not the absence of pain—it was the decision to remain present in the middle of it.

There are moments in life when everything in you wants to run—out of the room, out of the conversation, out of the truth rising inside you. I've had moments where I wanted to withdraw completely, to close the door, to avoid what felt too heavy or too sharp to face. Moments when staying felt uncomfortable, vulnerable, or impossible.

But I've noticed something: when I stay—not in a forced way, but in a quiet, honest way—something begins to shift. Not immediately. Not dramatically. Sometimes staying simply means taking one steady breath instead of pulling away. Sometimes it looks like sitting in silence rather than shutting down. Sometimes it means letting myself feel the ache without rushing to escape it.

There was a day when I held a difficult truth I didn't want to acknowledge. Everything in me wanted to distract myself, numb myself, outrun the discomfort. But instead, I stayed with it for just a moment longer than usual. I didn't solve anything. I didn't feel brave. But by staying, even briefly, I realized I could hold more than I thought. That moment didn't make the situation easier—but it made me steadier.

Staying doesn't mean you have all the answers. It means you're choosing not to abandon yourself. That is the quiet courage of the Magdalene Path: the willingness to remain present long enough for truth to speak.

Affirmation

"I stay with myself, even when the moment feels hard."

Journaling Prompt

Where in your life have you wanted to run, hide, or withdraw? What would it feel like to stay with yourself for just one more breath, one more moment, one small step longer?

SECTION 3 — Devotion That Trembles

Not all devotion is steady.
Some days it shakes in your hands,
quivers in your breath,
and feels like a fragile thread
you're trying desperately to hold.
But trembling devotion
is still devotion.
What matters is not how strong you feel—
but that something in you
keeps reaching toward the light.

People often imagine devotion as unwavering—a serene calm, a confident faith, a heart that never falters. But real devotion is far more human than that. Mary's devotion wasn't perfect or polished. It lived in the tremble of grief, in the uncertainty of the unknown, in the ache of showing up even when her heart was breaking.

I've had days when devotion felt almost impossible—when my prayers were scattered thoughts, when my patience was thin, when fear pressed against my ribs so tightly it was hard to breathe. Days when my version of devotion looked like simply getting out of bed, or whispering a small "help me," or placing a hand over my heart because I didn't know what else to do.

There was an evening when everything inside me felt tangled. I tried to meditate, but my mind was loud. I tried to ground myself, but my chest was tight. I felt frustrated that I couldn't "feel spiritual," as if devotion should rise in me like a warm glow on command. I remember thinking, "Why can't I be calmer? Why can't I feel centered?" And then the gentlest realization came: devotion isn't about performance. It isn't about feeling peaceful or enlightened. Sometimes devotion is simply staying connected to yourself while you shake. Sometimes it's letting the tears come. Sometimes it's acknowledging, "I'm overwhelmed, but I'm here."

Trembling devotion is still devotion.

Mary did not walk her path without fear. She walked it with fear in her body and courage in her breath. She stayed. She returned. She kept showing up—not because she felt strong, but because something deeper than fear was guiding her.

Your devotion doesn't need to be steady to be sacred. It only needs to be honest.

Affirmation

"My devotion counts, even when it trembles."

Journaling Prompt

Write about a moment when you showed up for yourself even though you felt shaky, overwhelmed, or unsure. What did that moment reveal about your courage?

SECTION 4 — Soft Strength: The Feminine Way of Holding Power

Strength does not always roar.
Sometimes it arrives as a quiet breath,
a steady gaze,
a choice not to collapse
when the heart feels tender.
Soft strength is not weakness—
it is power wrapped in gentleness,
courage woven through compassion,
truth spoken without force.
It is the strength Mary carried
in the palm of her hand.

Mary Magdalene's strength was not the hardened kind the world often celebrates. It wasn't loud or aggressive or armored. Her strength was soft—rooted in presence, intuition, steadiness, and the willingness to remain open even when life tried to close her. This kind of strength is often misunderstood. People mistake softness for fragility, or gentleness for passivity. But soft strength is one of the hardest forms of courage because it requires you to stay connected to yourself instead of shutting down.

I've had moments when I felt the pull to harden—to defend myself, to push back, to match someone else's intensity with my own. It felt safer to tighten than to stay open. But each time I reacted that way, something inside me felt off, like I was stepping out of alignment with who I truly am.

There was a conversation once where I felt myself bracing—shoulders tight, jaw clenched, heart retreating. I wanted to shut down emotionally, to end the discussion, to protect myself by closing. But something within me whispered, "Soften, just enough." So I took a breath. I let my shoulders drop. I didn't force anything. I didn't pretend I wasn't hurt or overwhelmed. I just allowed myself to stay present without armoring.

And in that small shift, the whole interaction changed. I wasn't powerless. I wasn't submissive. I was simply rooted in myself in a way that didn't require walls. That softness wasn't passive—it was powerful. It allowed me to speak clearly without reacting from fear. It helped me hold my boundaries with grace instead of defensiveness.

Soft strength isn't about being agreeable or silent. It's about choosing truth without aggression, presence without collapse, boundaries without bitterness. It's about remaining yourself in the moments when it would be easier to harden.

This is the Magdalene way of power: strength that doesn't need to shout, because it rises from within.

Affirmation

"My softness is strength. My presence is power."

Journaling Prompt

When have you chosen softness instead of shutting down or hardening? What did that moment show you about your own strength?

SECTION 5 — The Voice That Rises in You

There is a voice inside you
that has waited years to be heard—
quiet at first,
like a small ripple beneath the surface,
then growing stronger
each time you choose truth
over pleasing,
presence over silence,
yourself over approval.
This is the voice Mary carried—
the one that cannot be erased.

Mary Magdalene knew what it felt like to have her voice questioned. In the Gospel accounts, Peter challenges her, doubts her, dismisses her clarity. Her wisdom didn't crumble under his skepticism—it strengthened. She didn't argue to be believed; she spoke from inner authority. She trusted the voice rising inside her, even when others could not hear it.

There have been times in my own life when my voice felt small. Times when I minimized what I felt, softened my truth to avoid conflict, or held back because I worried someone might misunderstand me. Sometimes I stayed silent because speaking felt unsafe. Other times I spoke but then questioned myself afterward, replaying the moment in my mind, wondering if I should have said less—or more.

There was a moment recently when I shared something honest and vulnerable. It wasn't dramatic or confrontational—just true. And when the conversation ended, a familiar wave of doubt swept over me: *Was I too much? Did I sound dramatic? Should I have stayed quiet?* But as the day went on, something gently shifted. I realized the trembling inside me wasn't a warning—it was a sign that I had spoken from a place that mattered. My voice wasn't loud, but it was real. And that truth needed space, even if it shook coming out.

Finding your voice isn't about becoming louder. It's about becoming clearer. It's about honoring what rises in you instead of pushing it down. It's about trusting the wisdom that speaks softly at first, then more steadily as you stop silencing it.

The Magdalene Path teaches that your voice is sacred—not because others validate it, but because it comes from your deepest knowing. When you speak from that place, you are not asking for permission. You are remembering who you are.

Affirmation

"My voice is rising, steady and true."

Journaling Prompt

What truth have you held inside because you feared being misunderstood, dismissed, or doubted? What would it feel like to give that truth a little more room to speak?

SECTION 6 — Healing That Doesn't Look Like Healing

Healing does not always look holy.
Sometimes it looks like crying in the shower,
like saying no when your voice shakes,
like resting when the world expects you to rise.
Sometimes healing feels like breaking,
because the old self is loosening its grip.
The path is not tidy—
but every unraveling
is clearing space for the new.

We tend to imagine healing as clarity, calm, and progress. We imagine ourselves growing softer, wiser, more peaceful as the inner work deepens. But real healing is far messier than that. Even Mary's path—steady as she was—led her through grief, confusion, loss, and moments that looked nothing like awakening from the outside.

There have been times when I thought I was going backwards because I felt overwhelmed, emotional, or exhausted. Times when I reacted in ways I wasn't proud of. Times when I needed more rest, more space, more gentleness than usual. And I remember thinking, *If I were truly healing, shouldn't I feel better than this? Stronger than this? More together?*

But healing often looks worse before it looks better. It brings to the surface what you've avoided. It releases emotions you've held for years. It asks you to tell inconvenient truths and to set boundaries that feel uncomfortable at first. It shakes loose what can't come with you into your next chapter.

There was a week not long ago when I felt off—tired, irritable, overly sensitive. I didn't recognize myself. At first, I thought I was failing my spiritual practices, like I had "fallen out" of alignment. But as the days passed, I realized something quieter was happening. Old patterns were surfacing, asking to be seen. The stress I had pushed aside was finally requesting to be acknowledged. I wasn't falling apart—I was shedding.

Sometimes the messy days are the proof that healing is working, not failing. Healing is a dismantling before it is a rebuilding. It is the body, the mind, and the soul cooperating in ways we can't always see.

The Magdalene Path honors healing in all its forms—not just the peaceful ones. Mary teaches us that wholeness is not a straight line. It is a rising and falling, a remembering and forgetting, a softening and opening again.

Affirmation

"I honor my healing, even when it feels messy."

Journaling Prompt

Write about a time when you thought you were "falling apart," only to realize later that something important was shifting or releasing. What was being healed beneath the surface?

SECTION 7 — The Heart That Knows Before the Mind Understands

The mind wants proof.
The heart wants truth.
One gathers facts,
the other gathers knowing.
And sometimes the heart steps forward first—
before the mind can catch up,
before the path makes sense,
before the pieces fit.
Trust the quiet pull within you.
It knows the way home.

One of Mary Magdalene's greatest strengths was her ability to recognize truth before it made sense. She didn't rely solely on logic or argument; she sensed, she felt, she knew. Her intuition wasn't mystical in a dramatic way—it was grounded, clear, and unmistakably hers.

There have been moments in my own life when my heart understood something long before my mind agreed. Times when I felt a subtle tug inside—a nudge to slow down, a whisper to pay attention, a discomfort I couldn't explain. My mind questioned it, analyzed it, tried to talk me out of it. But the feeling stayed.

There was a decision I wrestled with for weeks. Every logical part of me said I should push forward, keep going, stay committed to what I'd already invested in. But my heart felt heavier each time I tried. It was an ache more than a message, a quiet unease that kept rising no matter how much I tried to rationalize it away. Eventually, after ignoring the feeling long enough, I finally paused and asked myself, *What if this discomfort is guidance? What if my heart knows something I haven't admitted yet?*

When I allowed myself to listen—not obey blindly, but truly listen—I realized the heaviness wasn't resistance. It was truth. The moment I acknowledged that, something inside me softened. The path didn't instantly become clear, but I could feel a deeper alignment returning, like I had stopped betraying myself.

Intuition is not dramatic. It's subtle, steady, and often inconvenient. It doesn't always give reasons—it gives direction. It shows up as a sense of unease, a quiet internal shift you can't explain, or a feeling of peace that arrives before understanding does. Sometimes it's a quiet yes or no when the mind wants a paragraph of explanation.

On the Magdalene Path, intuition is not an accessory—it's a compass. Mary trusted the knowing beneath the knowing, the truth that rises before understanding arrives.

You don't need to understand something for your heart to recognize it fully. Your mind will catch up later. Let your heart go first.

Affirmation

"My heart knows the truth, even before my mind understands it."

Journaling Prompt

Think of a time when your intuition spoke before logic did. What did your heart know—and what happened when you finally listened?

SECTION 8 — Rising Before Dawn

The darkest hours
are not the ones without light—
they are the ones
where you must rise
without knowing
what waits ahead.
Mary walked into the morning
before the sun returned,
before hope made sense,
before she knew
what she would find.
Sometimes rising
is the bravest thing you do.

Mary was the first to the tomb—before the others, before certainty, before clarity. She didn't wait for the sun. She didn't wait until she felt strong or sure. She went because something within her whispered, *Go*. Not because she understood, but because her heart refused to stay still.

There have been mornings when I, too, had to rise before I felt ready. Days when I woke with heaviness, uncertainty, or fear lingering from the night before. Days when I wanted to hide under the covers—not out of laziness, but because the world felt too sharp to touch. And yet something in me—soft but persistent—nudged me to get up, to open the door to the day, to take one small step forward.

There was a particular morning when I woke long before sunrise for no reason I could explain. My thoughts were scattered, my emotions tired, and the last thing I wanted was to face anything. I sat on the edge of the bed for a long time, feeling suspended between wanting to stay in the dark and knowing I needed to move. Eventually, I stood. Not with energy or motivation—just willingness. I made tea. I stared out the window. I breathed. And slowly, something inside me loosened. Not a breakthrough—just a sense that I had chosen myself, even in the dimness.

Rising before dawn doesn't always mean waking early. Sometimes it means choosing hope before you see the evidence. Sometimes it means taking a step when all you have is the strength to lift your foot. Sometimes it means trusting that the light will come, even if you can't feel it yet.

Mary teaches that dawn is not something you wait for—it's something you walk toward. Not with certainty, but with devotion. You rise because something in you refuses to stay in the place where fear left you. You rise because your soul knows the sun will meet you halfway.

Affirmation

"I rise gently, even when the dawn feels far away."

Journaling Prompt

Write about a time when you took a step before you felt ready. What helped you rise? And what shifted once you did?

SECTION 9 — Loving Without Losing Yourself

Love is not meant to drown you,
shrink you, or pull you away
from your own center.
True love holds space—for truth,
for breath, for the sacred ground
beneath your feet.
Love is not the abandoning of yourself.
It is the returning to who you are
even as you open your heart to another.

Mary Magdalene loved deeply, but she did not disappear inside her devotion. She walked beside the Teacher, not behind him. Her love strengthened her instead of diminishing her, grounded her instead of scattering her. That is sacred love: connection without collapse, devotion without erasure, tenderness that does not erase the self.

There have been times in my life when I misunderstood what love required of me. Times when I softened too much, bent too far, or made myself smaller so someone else could feel comfortable. Times when I stayed silent to keep the peace, or absorbed more than my heart could hold because I thought it made me loyal or kind. It took me a long time to recognize that shrinking myself wasn't love—it was fear wearing a softer face.

There was a relationship where I felt I slowly started losing my sense of self without even realizing it. I agreed to things that I didn't necessarily want to do. I minimized my needs. I convinced myself that holding everything together was my responsibility. And when I finally stepped back and truly looked at what I had become, I barely recognized myself. My voice was quieter. My energy was dimmer. My boundaries were soft to the point of dissolving. Ending that pattern wasn't easy—it felt like unlearning an entire language. But the moment I chose to return to myself, the fog began to lift. I could breathe again. I could hear my own thoughts again. I could feel my own heart again.

The Magdalene Path teaches that love is a shared rising, not a slow disappearance. Love that asks you to abandon yourself is not love. Love that asks you to betray your own truth is not devotion. Love that dims your voice is not sacred.

Sacred love:

- makes room for your truth
- honors your boundaries
- expands both hearts
- allows both souls to stand tall
- brings you closer to yourself, not farther away

Mary teaches that loving another begins with loving yourself—not selfishly, but wisely. The more grounded you are in who you are, the more love you are capable of giving and receiving. Love and selfhood are not opposites; they are companions on the same path.

Affirmation

"I love without losing myself. My heart and my truth belong together."

Journaling Prompt

Reflect on a time when you lost parts of yourself in the name of love—romantic, familial, or otherwise. What would it look like to love while staying rooted in your own truth?

SECTION 10 — Becoming the Rose: Your Path Forward

You are not who you were
when you first stepped onto this path.
Something in you has softened,
something in you has strengthened,
and something in you has begun to bloom
in ways you cannot yet see.
Becoming is not sudden.
It is a slow unfurling—
petal by petal,
truth by truth,
breath by breath.
You are opening,
and that is enough.

Mary Magdalene's path was not defined by a single moment. It was a journey of unfolding—of rising, returning, realigning, remembering. She did not become a symbol of devotion in one great act; she became who she was through countless small choices: to stay, to soften, to trust, to rise, to speak, to love.

Your path is the same.

You do not need to transform overnight. You do not need to have everything figured out. Becoming the rose is about returning to yourself again and again, even when life feels overwhelming or unclear.

There have been times in my own journey when I thought I wasn't growing because I couldn't see the change. I felt stuck, tired, or unsure, and I assumed that meant I was failing somehow. But looking back, those were often the seasons when the deepest shifts were taking root beneath the surface. Growth doesn't always announce itself. Sometimes it looks like rest. Sometimes it feels like uncertainty. Sometimes it feels like nothing is happening at all.

There was a stretch of time when I felt disconnected from everything—my creativity, my intuition, my sense of purpose. I went through the motions, doing what needed to be done, but I felt flat inside. Months later, something small and unexpected stirred in me. A thought. A spark. A quiet sense of possibility. And I realized, with some surprise, that I had been growing the whole time. I wasn't failing. I was preparing.

Becoming the rose means trusting the pace of your own unfolding. It means honoring your seasons—your blooming and your resting, your clarity and your questions. It means allowing your heart to open at its own tempo without forcing outcomes or rushing the process.

Mary's story reminds us that the path of the heart is not linear. You will rise and fall. You will remember and forget.

You will soften and tighten and soften again. None of this is wrong. All of it is becoming.

You are becoming the rose not because you are perfect, but because you are willing. Because you continue to return. Because something in you keeps moving toward the light, even when the light feels far away.

This willingness is your path forward. This devotion is your awakening. This unfolding is your sacred becoming.

Affirmation

"I trust the pace of my unfolding. I am becoming the rose, one breath at a time."

Journaling Prompt

What part of you is beginning to open, soften, or awaken— quietly, subtly, even if you can't fully see it yet? Write about the ways you are becoming, even in your gentlest steps.

Closing Blessing

May you walk with the courage of the Magdalene,
steady even when your heart trembles,
present even when the world feels loud,
rooted even when the path is unclear.
May you honor your rising—
the small ones,
the quiet ones,
the ones no one else sees
but your soul recognizes instantly.

May your softness become your strength,
your truth become your compass,
and your devotion become the light
that guides you gently home to yourself.

May the whispers of your heart
speak louder than your fear.
May the wisdom within you
meet you in every step.
And may each moment of returning
be a reminder that you are never lost—
only unfolding.

Go with remembrance.
Go with gentleness.
Go with the rose blooming in your chest,
one petal at a time.

PUBLICATIONS BY ROOTED HOUND PRESS

The Rose Series™ — Pocket Sanctuaries

The Rose Codex
Mary Magdalene: A Sanctuary of Remembrance
The Magdalene Path
(Additional titles forthcoming)

Pocket Sanctuary Series™

Whispers from the Soul
The Test That I Refused
(Future mini-sanctuaries coming soon)

Books by Rooted Hound Press

Returning to Wholeness: An Invitation to the Soul
Echoes Through the Spiral: A Soul's Continuum
Healing the Past Through the Present
Encoded in Stone: The Memory of Earth & The Story of Us
Thoth & the Tablets: A Journey Through the Crystalline Codes
The Adventures of Layla and Lilly (Children's Series)

Journals & Companions

Rooted Reflections Journal
The Rose Journal
Celestial Journal
Floral Journal
(Additional themed journals coming soon)

Published by
Rooted Hound Press
Vienna, New Jersey
www.rootedhoundpress.com